# Rookie
## Read-About® Health

# Tasting

## By Sharon Gordon

**Consultants**
Nanci R. Vargus, Ed.D.
Primary Multiage Teacher
Decatur Township Schools, Indianapolis, Indiana

Jan Jenner, Ph.D.

Children's Press®
A Division of Scholastic Inc.
New York   Toronto   London   Auckland   Sydney
Mexico City   New Delhi   Hong Kong
Danbury, Connecticut

Designer: Herman Adler Design
Photo Researcher: Caroline Anderson
The photo on the cover shows a young girl eating a banana split.

**Library of Congress Cataloging-in-Publication Data**

Gordon, Sharon.
    Tasting / by Sharon Gordon.
       p. cm. — (Rookie read-about health)
    Includes index.
    Summary: This simple introduction to the sense of taste discusses how
we taste the things we eat.
    ISBN 0-516-22293-7 (lib. bdg.)    0-516-25992-X (pbk.)
    1. Taste—Juvenile literature. [1. Taste. 2. Senses and sensation.] I. Title.
II. Series.
QP456 .G67    2001
612.8'7—dc21

                                  00-060215

What is your favorite
way to eat a banana?
How do you know?

You know because of your sense of taste.

Tasting is one of the five senses. The others are hearing, seeing, touching, and smelling.

The sense of taste begins with your tongue.

# Look in the mirror and stick out your tongue.

Your tongue is covered with little bumps. Each bump is filled with many taste buds.

The taste buds on the tip of your tongue taste salty and sweet things.

The taste buds on the sides taste sour things.

And the back of your tongue has taste buds for bitter things.

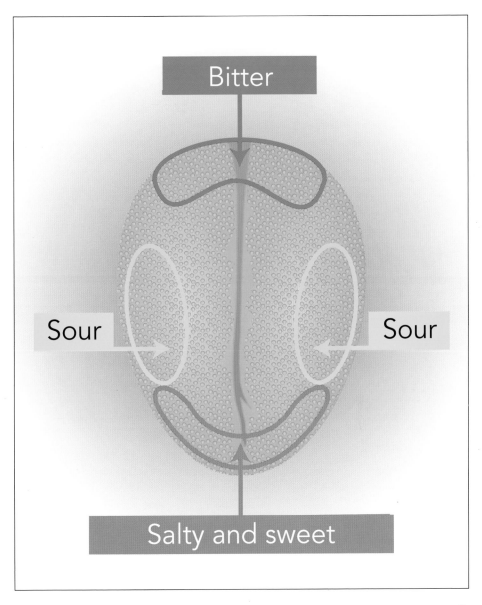

9

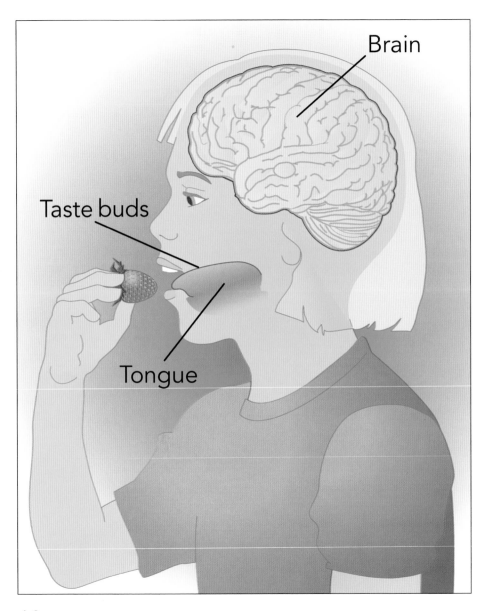

Brain

Taste buds

Tongue

10

The taste buds tell your brain what you are tasting.

Then your brain tells you if you like what you are eating or drinking.

That is how you taste things.

# A picnic is a good place to try out your taste buds.

You will find lots of good food to taste.

Try the sweet corn.
Do you like it plain or
with some melted butter?

Taste a sour pickle.
What a face!

Look at all the salads.
There is something for
every taste.

Try some cheese. Each one
tastes very different.

This juicy watermelon
looks good to eat.
Watch out for the seeds!

Would you like some
of these salty chips?

Many grown-ups like
the taste of bitter coffee.
Do you?

If a lemon is sour, why is lemonade so sweet?

The secret is lots of sugar!

Do not eat food that
has been sitting in the
sun too long.

It is always best to throw it away. It could make you sick.

# Desserts can be very sweet.

Would you like fresh
strawberries or an ice
cream cone? Both!

How would you describe the taste of this?

Yummy!

# Words You Know

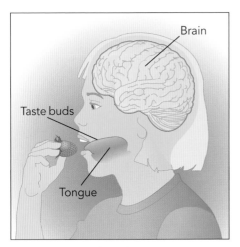

brain

bitter

salty

sour

sweet

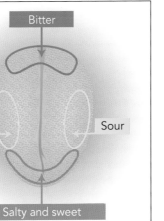

taste buds

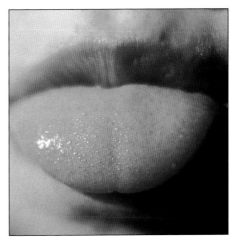

tongue

# Index

# About the Author

Sharon Gordon is a writer living in Midland Park, New Jersey. She and her husband have three school-aged children and a spoiled pooch. Together they enjoy visiting the Outer Banks of North Carolina as often as possible.

# Photo Credits

Photographs ©: Envision: 16 (Osentoski & Zoda); Nance S. Trueworthy: 15, 17, 19, 25, 30 bottom, 31 top left; Photo Researchers, NY/Dennis Purse: 3 top right; PhotoEdit: 3 bottom left (Mary Kate Denny), 12 (Myrleen Ferguson Cate), cover (Felicia Martinez), 3 top left, 3 bottom right, 22 (Michael Newman), 26 (Robin L. Sachs), 27, 31 top right (D. Young-Wolff); Rigoberto Quinteros: 5, 6; Stock Boston: 24 (Bill Bachmann), 13 (Steven Frame), 28 (Jean-Claude Lejeune); Stone: 14 (Sara Gray), 7, 31 bottom right (Roy Gumpel);Viesti Collection, Inc.: 21, 30 top right (M.G. Perelli/Ask Images), 18 (Robert Winslow).

Illustrations by Patricia Rasch.